Welcome to the Museum of Cattle

POEMS BY

JANE ORMEROD

THREE ROOMS PRESS

NEW YORK CITY

Grateful acknowledgement is made to the editors of the journals below for publishing the following poems, which sometimes appeared in different forms.

Beat the Dust, Polarity, The Rutherford Red Wheelbarrow,
Sparring With Beatnik Ghosts, Spiny Babbler

Welcome to the Museum of Cattle

All contents Copyright © 2012 by Jane Ormerod

All rights reserved. No part of this book may be reproduced without permission of the author or publisher, except for brief quotes for review purposes. For permissions, please write to editor@threeroomspress.com.

Editor: Peter Carlaftes

Cover and Interior Design:
Kat Georges Design, New York, NY
katgeorges.com

First Edition

ISBN: 978-0-9835813-9-0

Printed in the United States of America.
Text set in Adobe Caslon.

Published by
Three Rooms Press, New York, NY
threeroomspress.com

CONTENTS

Lying Sideways, Eyes Closed, Rain 1

Alvin Says Buy Nuts 4

Do You Know of Pains That Do Not Smell? 7

Call Me a Cabernet Sauvignon 9

The Second Rebecca 12

Vernacular of the Untitled 15

Contamination 17

Breathless Around Roadworks 19

Asphalt Drifter 22

Among the Dead 25

Leasing a Phantom 28

Initial Notes for a Possibly Punk Poem About—
at the Moment—a Girl Called Lucy 31

Lacking Energy for Further Events,
Marion Licks Stamps 33

Was Bartholomew a Stranger or Strangler? 35

The Killing 38

The Young and Innocent Ride Again 41

Dead Man's Dog 44

What Shall We Do About Lunch,
You Carnival Wife? 49

Harness 52

Or Indeed Any Alcohol 54

Impact and Scar (To Go) 57

Analyze This ~~(2008)~~ Redux 60

Within This Progression, Warmth 62

In memory of Brant Lyon – because, because, because.

Heartfelt thanks and love to Pete,
and to all my wonderful family and friends
in the new, the old, and the other worlds.

Welcome to the Museum of Cattle

Lying Sideways, Eyes Closed, Rain

A June   an empty June
of streets   a June   bay horse's leg
salt tapers   hairpins   hatpins   bending songs
There is a fish
of bibs   no air   nor hands
There is a fish   a face   there is an oar
No handles   blouse
A turret   mother   wash abandoned
Northern wheatear wind to scale

There is a scarf for little horse
Bedtime slurp for little horse
Bread for breath   hunk for horse
Remember little, little horse
Remember horsey, little horse?

Not very far, not very far
Not very far to go
Hup hup!
Not very far, not very far
Not very far to go
Hup hup!

Newborn clouds   wild
angled nails to jamboree   blot room of ink
Hunk bread random laces tankard stone

Please come in
Please come in
Please come in
Please come in

Children ripping legs from secrets
Girls   smoking pipe trails   old-style lake
Limb of mutton sleeve   straw straw   the air in Malmö
Twin games   kitchen   pantry
That man and her of him ago and long I do I do
or buried close   indeed   whitebell
Standing here with folded letter   nosewipe pipesmoke
Hup! Hup!

Ainmount ainmount ainmount
Bluryellow bluryellow bluryellow
So long so long so long so long so long

Please   come in
I, the old man old who always almost never weeps
Two large horses   a where-you-art-from Guernsey heifer
Where? Whence? Whence?
Doctor or linguist   modern biological
Remove   remove
then microscope
these eyes

Yes-please-do's
A fellow with no signature   yes
Indeed yes   try again yes
Say horsey   say yes, little horsey
Withdraw your name   your birth place   birth date
mother's maiden
Spit out spit out spit out spit out spit out spit out
Obsolete unlearn   scrub-a-dub to nothing

Can you say *blunt instrument*?
Can you say *prayer*?
The picture of the smiling Christ?
Forget-me-not?
Treatise?
Other things?

Put down   put it down!
This is your hand   this is your arm
This is your shoulder   this is your cap
This is your blade
Rrr rrr rrr
Do you respond to feigned trust?
Joist!

Ainmount ainmount ainmount

The air in Malmö sleeps
Hook and tenter more this balance moment
A58 832

Babe and hare to rock to sleep
Charmed to meet you charmed to sleep
Two little horses rock to sleep
Pencil and cavalry rock to sleep

Not very far and not very far
Not very far to go
Huh huh
Not very far so not very far
Not very far to go
Uh huh

Close your eyes
Remember our talk?

This is your tree frog moment
Snatch the reins, Sir
Gallantly ride

HUP HUP HUP

Alvin Says Buy Nuts

Depicted in fictitious speed, intrepid
Same old visor, shirt sleeves
A daily game of concrete bugaboo
High-yield war-preventive crops
"Good Morning, Globe," says Alvin

Twilight sages and futurists
Feudal bedevillers saving breath
Hats stand round the helm of Europe
Scrap the intelligence—
News is diggable, facts not pumpable
"Ha ha ha ha ha," says Alvin

Crowds make me nervous, knees too
A logistical idea of scotch and soda,
jitters and organs
Milk has poison, babies have poison
"Good Morning, Globe," says Alvin

Exactly.
London in sunshine—*ha!*—is a very fine man
Look at the birds, mister, and places for birds
And feeding the birds is dandy dandy dandy
Dandy as a lion

Exactly.
My Milords, my Miladies, my Royal Britannia hearties—
I trust exuberance to clear movement and epitaphs
Unfamiliar with cheese, machinery, and Rembrandt,
well-meaning amateurs believe in large families

Teapot villages, unreliable wind-turning mills
Signals to demand a romantic haywain, mud streaks, tall grass, short
A quick play of bridge or cribbage with police
Snooping with the wrong way sailors, the hat creators
Piecemeal disguised as a plate, pope, or pirate
Hot Hell Europe in a dressing-down robe
Price of a hypocrite is not dead— they gave it to me, who was not me
was a substitute man who looked like me. Yes,
consider the facts of their hands and can hardly think the telling
of the birds in the city is the man with the stare and the swing
of a rain jacket, half of a hell of an hour
Dad's Army. Tabloid

Good Morning, Alvin
Say Good Morning to the world

Chain shadow papers
Having fun with crackpots, window cleaners, foggy duck materializers
Waiting in the room-gloom for gentlemen
you really should prefer to avoid
Please don't come bother with tulips
And no signs yet of a deck and a chat that I beg of an argument evidently
with a touch of the cap and a spot of the breakfast for the assassin
that impossible in a sweater that is a . . . (quiet boy quiet!)
Horse Guards, fireguards, guardians of nerves, nicely
convenient capsules or boats to cap or upsize
A few muzzled moments is inspiration for a story involving
a private detective named Roly

"Oh! What a nice example of cathedratic architecture, sir."
"How about a trip up north, sir? Up top, up close?"

There goes another
Blood and smallpox
High neck sweaters, tramps who appear ridiculous to the unwary,
politicians who are genial, and the weather is—as ever—permissive
Nothing doing arms to faint into and are you alone
and can you talk and count and trill *hello!*
into a phone already dead?
May I use your potato flood-lighting, Alvin?
May I? May I?
Alvin, may I say hello?

Birth oars
This isn't bad melody or target practice under the wing with pearls
and a pilot and fools to wash away the tiptop steers
in slaughterhouses and first-class stagecoaches
and a lot of prime and personal history
that today seems dated
Paper cutouts of a giant man on a small bicycle
Nailing the door to an exit, the bad guy stretches his single leg

*

Alvin says buy nuts
Buy more than you need
Bury them
In the spring you can sell

Do You Know of Pains That Do Not Smell?

Do you know of pains that do not smell?

There are steps, directions on top of steps, and further steps. A man carrying a fedora or saint up the steps. Directions to the Pacific, to Quebec. Directions, curtains, and beads. A coat to carry.

Who is there? You have a candle. You have a tie. Is it this time of night? May you help in any way? Can you save your life so hard, it cracks apart a lie? Do you know of pains that do not smell?

To tell. To place around your next. What you cannot imagine, you cannot remember. No one knows the day is unattended. On Wednesdays you work the garden, leave the ladder and morning behind. The painting and the smell of pain. Do you know of pains that do not smell?

The bicycle does not always fall. The horse is unaware of the tire.

When you return, you will patch the tire *and* the morning. A man without carpentry carrying a hat. A man without chamber. Do you confess to Quebec?

You discovered the body and called the police and were told you could leave. And you don't know what to do. Is there another way? Have you ever been afraid of anything? Not been good? Achieved pity for pity's sake? The tire was not so flat after all. Nothing dropped, no girls, all walls spotless. Why confess to anyone?

And is it convenient? How far can you push the bicycle? Will you wash it? Polish? Accessorize? Ring ding ding ding. One detail jumps to another. This is accomplishment.

Where were you at eleven o'clock?
You appear deeply sorrowed.
Do you know of pains that smell of paint?
Where were you at eleven?

Track down the crown prosecutor. Balance a crystal tumbler on his forehead. Tell his wife, *what beautiful shoulder detail!* Murder is not taken by strides. You will find lettuce, you will find pain. You ought to be in bed with a thriller.

Do you confess? Do you confess?

Is it peaceful lying with the dead? Are you in love with the never-should-be-seen? Have you questioned who you are? There is a small boy in a cardigan inside us all. There is smoke. There is want and pretend and Quebec continues to exist.

Do you confess? Do you see and believe things as they are? Pity is bothersome but ferries seem often embarrassing.

Do you confess? You grew up together, fell in love. She wore a white dress like she was already a widow. Dancing that evening, how many times did she think of herself? Always yearning the brilliant. A lovely day. The end of summer. A storm so sudden, you sheltered in the gazebo. Wherever you go, whatever the date, it remains five years ago.

Do you hope truth is established? You gave them what was needed. Will flowers help? Will kneeling? Hand over the radio, the flowers. Do you digest or direct traffic? Do you use your bicycle? Have you had lunch? Hold this hand between the flowers. Prize apart this life. The flowers will fit neatly in the trunk.

Call a doctor for evidence not cure. This is a night of murder. There is distance. There is light. There is kneeling. Go back and then leave.

How is life in Quebec? This time of night, do you truly experience direction? You were costumed as a sailor and he was a priest and you shared a burger and he was method, oh yes. Do you know of smells that do not pain?

How did you use to paint? Oh, yes. Left to right, or right to left? Did you cope with ladders? Would he have looked up at this point? Towards the people, or architecture, or whatever else might be there? He didn't, but would you? Are you a human, being inspected? Are you openly romantic? Some choose reason, others faith. Both fail. (Boom.) Love is a technocrat. Are you a Dolly or an Alma? Would you give all this up for cartoons? The skin of your teeth? A smile from Montgomery Clift? Do any of us really, truly, deserve to live in Quebec?

Call Me a Cabernet Sauvignon

You buy a box   You sell a box
You buy a box   You sell a box

Milk cartons   Bottle assembly lines
Kindling   Tree-light   Languor
A million hushes louder than one single snore
Adding infinity and removing the now and never
and possibly will
Anatomical amoroso   Knotweed
Boats entering blanks and exiting drawn-out mess

You buy a box   You sell a box   You bail a box
The lake   The kidneys   Lies the space between ten folds
Slice of lime horizon   The Park Café
The lure of the fail   of the foals
The respect of dew
Steal a box and then seal a box
Parasitical   Hysterical   *Mess*

Mess   Painlessness   Numberless   Lustration   *Mess*
Tape across the gorge

STOP   WET PAINT   YIELD   YIELD

Elvis does not care where you live
The wall is in the soil!   The wall is hidden inside the soiled!
Listen!   Can you hear the shut-the-fuck of bear bells?
She was twisted by that Beatles band

Buy a box!   Sell a box!
The sound of his body   Ranger Lynne
Polytechnicals   Moggies in limbo   Hopscotching experts
Power talkers   Drinkers with a view to a rue

They are all here!
They are all here!

Broadsheet rumors   Tourist trout hatcheries   WET PAINT
Mule hostelries   Distilleries   Celery de-stringers
South Dakota ladies with tractor skirts and courtesy

WET PAINT   WET PAINT

Sprinkling of small town in the city
Count the spots you cannot change   Erase the rest
Jeopardy   Property
Dog control   Reconciliation
The basin for condemned men to wash their final faces

WET PAINT   WET PAINT

Propriety   Sell and buy and pry and prize
Twisted by that Beatles band

WET PAINT   WET PAINT

Fertility of travelers!   Ranger Lynne!   The Damsel Tavern
Pretty pretty pretty   Pretty pretty pretty
Buy the box   Bury the box   Lactate   Lactate

WET PAINT   WET PAINT

The lunge to the bank and the branch and the arm
that might just just just be long long long enough
if you were but a little older older taller

WET PAINT   WET PAINT

At high school your father joined the cheese club
At night school he grew fat with sleep
Can you spend your life as a river?   A chord?
A dip in the ground?   Mustard?
Can you resist nature from the gnat through the gold finch
and the fish to the all of the mighty?
May you like to lick the paint before it has fully dried?

DIGBY   THE BIGGEST DOG IN THE WORLD!

Divulge the first color you remember
Maybe then we will all become happy

The Second Rebecca

Picturization.
Lumsden Hare.
Advancing.

Fingers on sell-by past.
A painter of trees. The same perfect tree.
How do you find Monte Carlo? Postcard quality?

Grapefruit 8 Pear 12 Apple 12
Banana 4 Oranges Mandarins
Omelette with Ham 9 Egg in Aspic 4

Ready. All these few last days. Those little demons to remember. Biting nails in front of charity stores and the car waiting at the door. Dressing in another room. You don't belong in that kind of you-know-what-I-mean world. And bless you for that. It's a pity you will grow up behind palm trees.

When did it start happening, this…this whirlwind? A foot, fast water, still water, and good luck catching that hat. A thousand perfectly lovely blooms. The British, when their hat blows away in the wind, say *Woo!* What do you say?

How do you do and how do you do it?

Go downstairs by first going up. Was Alice satisfactory? She will admit you once a week to the public.

Fried Eggs with Tomato Sauce
Boiled Eggs with Croutons 9
Plate of Eggs with Sausages 9

Thank you for yesterday. There's a thrilling article in *The Times* mentioning cricket, I believe.

Do you use the morning room after breakfast? Do you know it is on the left? I have been dead for over a year but I will approve the menu and then thank you and write letters like a marquis or a duke and I am not fluffy and I am fluffy and I am not fluffy and I am fluffy and I am not fluffy and I am fluffy and I am not fluffy and I am fluffy and I am not fluffy and I am fluffy.

I am tiresome and typical and a tricky girl and a how do you do. Are you an oil painting? She has nothing to do but ride or masquerade or torment a wind or give hoot to a notice. How funny you are. Like a child. Like a dog bought for a child. Like a walk down to a cove with a little sand and large rocks and a cottage and a door and it is rude to name him fool or ignoramus.

I suppose beauty may be seen from London.

Trouble is valuable. Cupid: an explanation of an idiot. A writing desk can often be mended. Are you an upstairs person, a prize cow, or a slap in the eye? Do you gossip about naivety, binoculars, or attractiveness? You ought to have married a terribly happy boy who loves answers from a girl in a black velvet bow that no one knows is attached to a tripod.

Drapes, fastenings. You always wanted to see this room, to be this room, to feel this expensive. Undergarments stitched by unspecific but specialized nuns at dawn. Parties where everyone beckons. Oh my. Oh woo.

You can see my hand.
You can have my hand.
Be gone, be a corridor. Do not be a mistaken.

Listen to the sea listen to the sea listen to the sea.

Have you ever seen a favorite painting hung at the top of the stairs? A strongman's prop left inside a car? A delicate fan beautifies the bosom. A hat enhances an entrance.

There is no shame in the faltering surprise of your life.

Are you an unclaimed woman? Are you a lie? Is it true? This precious luckiest life with grandchildren and triumphs built from dirt and honor.

How funny. How perfect. What a delicious thrill. Are you smiling? Triumphant? Are you falling onto ship's tackle? Will you smile when you are dead? Will there be a moon? A cabin? Perhaps a dinghy?

Will you sink when you are dead? Will there be rain? An explanation of golf? A routine, out of the ordinary or otherwise? Reconditioning, check.

There is no reason for holes.

Lose your temper in a bed of pink-red roses with a bad big wolf with a touch of solicitude and a drumstick marinated with play. Is it totally worth your while? This is not a come come come come colonel major time.

There are still a few weeks to discover a motive. A nutshell inside a shepherds bush. A lovely girly child. (No softy words necessary.)

It is impossible to thank you.

Novelty breaks dawn. Distance bones to splinter to flame.
Valves are tight and you are the star.
Place your sister in the depth of the crowd and film your reaction.
Everyone sinks. Everyone dreams of Monte Europe.
Who now remembers the Lumsden Hare?

Vernacular of the Untitled

the light appears an arm a light appears an arm the light appears an arm a light appears an arm the light appears an arm a light appears an arm the light appears an arm a light appears an arm the light appears an arm a light appears an arm the light appears an arm a light appears an arm the light appears an arm a light appears an arm the light appears an arm a light appears an arm the light appears an arm

chair
sore eye
sorry
release possibility
air air air airrr airrr airrrr
replace

dirt-tan river-sound building / dirt-tan river-sound building / dirt-tan river-sound building / herd mind numb / herd mind numb / dirt-tan river-sound building / voices compete / in woodpecker crescendo / ditch-water-brown-sound-building / mind ber / dinge numb / light

forced through a slit
chronic / salt

wet greasy sullen gruesome endless arm of sky / fog / wet greasy sullen gruesome endless arm of sky / fog / near identical little shots of near identical interiors / near identical little shots of near identical interiors / near identical little shots of near identical interiors / near identical little shots of near identical buildings / wet greasy sullen arm of light appearing / white greasy sullen army of light appearing / stroll / emer-amber-ald / the lake a never-closing eye / the lake a never-closing eye / thin grey strolling bone bleach lawn arm slope of sky migratory / how thin how light / how light how thin / how light how thin / how light how near how

breeze slammed
there is center and essential
there are arms and light-song of finch
the enlightened and the entitled
pour impossibility with the implausible

shake / the light appears an arm / ricochet / the light appears the arm / ricochet / a light the arm a light the arm the light an arm a light an arm a light an arm the light appease an arm appease / shake / richochet / alarm alight alight alight alight alarm alarm alarm alarm alarm alarm the light a light appears an arm unfolding / richochet / a light unfolding / an arm unfolding / the light refolding / shake

unfolded whistle
crumpleskin
half-light
bird son
tint

veer / identical / veer / historical / near identical / grey grey grey grey grey / ricochet / interior / alarm alight alight alight alight alarm alarm alarm alarm alarm alarm / the light appears an arm unfolding

sore eye
possibility of space identity

fog light / dirt-tan river-sound salt crescendo / grade crescendo / mitigate / grade / grade / mitigate / dirt-tan river-sound near descending / alarm descending / light descending / again descending / ricochet / an arm appears / ricochet / an arm appears / ricochet / the light descends identical / the arm descends identical / the light a never-closing eye / the eye a never-ending lake / mitigate / air air air airrr / air descending / air air airrr / never-closing air air air airrr / air air air airrr / air air air airrr / air air air airrr / air descending / light descending / near-identical little shots of air / light descending / air descending / never-ending shots of air / of air / of air / of airrrrrrr / of airrrrrrrr.

Contamination

Do you travel by arrangement?
Tip your hat at the perfectly shod?
Here is the father you will soon plead to kill

Instrumental eyeglasses
A turn for the worst and the possible
Trappings, goose droppings, matchbooks, scotch
and plain old water. Baited legs, a premature
announcement in the papers, immature swing
of an arm. A father who hates with all the cash,
vernacular, and culpability in the world
Guilt runs faster than delight

He is the father who begs both pardon and question
Who will rarely chat to a tennis player eating lamb chops
Who knows about people he has never met
and those you have never heard of
You are the heel, sole, and tricksy step of the playmate
You are the mother's frillies and highballs
You are the needless to say
The two hour wait at a bus stop with a cigar,
newspaper, some wasted perambulation
Interest always vested, suited, mono

Do you travel by arrangement?
Keep a European train schedule on your desk?
Did she file them just a smidgeon too short?
Why grip the reins when you are not moving?
Does the band always play on?
Did you even enter the Magic Isle?

Maybe you hold plans for later . . .
To call a cop, a doctor, help the elderly cross the street
Love your stirring hound like a child, or a goat, a cheese,
a log, an ice-box, a goal to get even

Huh huh huh, huh huh huh
Is your name well yes?

So how would you do it, Mrs. Cunningham?
How in the world would you do it?
Everything important fits about the neck

Mrs. Cunningham, we are both indecent
With what manner shall we proceed?
Share a nip of sleep?
Shake the pearls? Dust off those glad rags?
Do we have cold feet to defrost?
A horse to debug?
A flower to smell from Mars?
I am the car pulling up. I am the hostage situation,
the sound seeping from your neighbor's headphones
Silk shadows dressing by the table, Ray's Danbury Diner

Help me, Mrs. Cunningham! Help me!
Are you a smoocher or are you simply educated?
How many more times can you change your name,
and then make-believe we do not notice
your personality is as crooked as ever?
Float to the ground like the lindy to cement

The richer you are, the smaller the teacup you drink from
I am your eyes now
There is undulation, a split of seemliness
The soothingness of paint
Allow someone else to crawl beneath the merry-go-round
Mrs. Cunningham, the arrow points in only one direction only
Mrs. Cunningham, draw yourself to here
This is the father of all nighttime
The sun remains a slut

Breathless Around Roadworks

22.275 and the trees and.

Lal la lal lal la and trees chant llll lllaaaa and trees whisper how she is dedicated to being such a small and local restaurant and being restrained.

Trees. Money? And trees. They interrupt. And then nice(ish) countryside to grow fonder of by the day.

Stuffed like quails and their tiny eggs and tinier legs, the wavers the brakes duh dud duh duh duh durrrr durrrr durrrrrr treesssss. She flails before lying.

Cathedrallaaaallla trees lllahahah cathedrallaaaallla *1.407* lllahahah cathedrallaaaa treeeeess llla lllahahah.

Not here. She lives here not <u>here</u>. Ham and eggs are how much? To whom? Okay…

May she enter? She has wiped her shoes with Sunday newspaper, finished her ham and eggs, mingled at the supermarket evening unofficial lonely-hearts. What is new? A discotheque? A drip? A script? A new assistant named Mandy? She would not mind anything at all. *79.9865.* Maybe we should pray for a random perhaps.

She has a loan. She has a tree. She is done being provocative and reasonably proactive. She has a baker's dozen number of thighs. She suffered a horribly late breakfast (in a back-to-front dress) of ham and mmmmmore more eggs.

What is she doing here? A chimp escaped from the zoological garden over a thousand kilometers away. The Saturday paper appeared better informed than the Sunday.

Does it matter she shares no fancy for the future? Does it matter if a line crosses sleep and money? Is that the pharmacy? There are others too, and others more. She switches buoyed and bored.

Prettier girls to see at noon, oh yes, but at 12:05 after kicking a corpse and fingerprinting a floozy, he shall see her and drink. And you? (Small chuckle.) Have you even noticed the envelope he slipped her last week? You are riding on a bet, on simple basic stay-in-the-ordinary trust. A fairly tall man, brown hair—a poor description. Full apologies. That is lazy. *7, 25, 400, 10.*

There is a tree and another.

She saw a guy killed in an accident. In her wallet I found a photo of an ambulance.

She saw a second class *3*, a rich man riding a bus, a good girl as lookout, a single . . . oh, whatever, whatever.

Who is a chicken? Who is a point? A moot? An operation? A hole to hide in when they removed her key. There is another tree and she is finding the place on the divan and may yet play a game of chess with the more intelligent of your neighbors.

There are further trees to come. Silver, lead, tooth-brushed, bog-bushed, roped and bandaged. Handed head over fist over heel and they stop her . . . rattattat *147.9.* . . from sharing. Trees speak to those pairs of Shire horses and cattle that strained and plodded in previous centuries.

And she is a hound on a gilt chair underneath that tree at a picnic or maybe a low-scale *193* celebration with fresh eggs and…let's say…fresh passion juice bellinis. Her sisters knit blankets for local and international charities but she cannot understand their texture and complicated theory of color. *147.2.* She wishes a detective would find her, unravel her plot from the knots and the haves and the sonorous. She is no place like home. You could call her a taxi, or rank, or rabbit, or a ramp that boats slide down, while the rest of you…well, you collect tickets, snap judgments. *2,000 8,000 9 8 1 zerrrrro 0 10,000 spot 4 oh ha.*

Trees watch corn flow, grass rests into dust. No tree is a precise size. Yellow ground. Dregs of plants. Bare wigwams of canes. Paint cracking round frames and sills. Sun reaching over yawns and night sweat.

Who is a chicken? What is a point? Again, who is this scumbaggage girl?

Blur of car park and lumber of white-roofed superstores. Tended verges. Lime trees. Tended verges. Lime trees. Lime trees. Illumination. Retching gargoyles and curls and blasts of food and people.

27.225. Seven hours, a straw-thin shot of river.

Cattthhhhhedtrallllllaaa tra laaaaaa tra laaaaaa laaaaahhhhhh. Ventilation, a hand-carved articulated cobra.

Listen.

The orange sky hangs over the scaffolded streets.

This may be the only face of human and irrepressible joy.

Asphalt Drifter

Enter for sardines, hard cheese, salami. For hot beef and fine pork, ham, fresh coffee, two eggs, a non-starting pistol, a radio increasing, nighttime necktie. Until. Slammed for danger.

Enough.
What time have you got?

There are morals, offences, cold feet turned backwards. It is, I maintain, your job to scare. To decide what to do, when to turn, and at what exact spot. Wager on horses or pyrotechnical disasters. Shift shapes to one side of the hallway. That is all. Some space still exists. That is all. Expected time of arrival 3:17 p.m. Until then slammed.

Lose and loose and alive and at large. Wear a clean shirt to watch the punks? It remains a habit for outside walls, but not much checking, not much. I'll be right back after you replace your spectacles and gaze once more at women and their foundation and fondness for scorpions.

What have you got for me today?

Swells come in bunches, that is all. Hang your hat, your head, your home. Filthy cats gnawing joints of diseased pseudo-chicken. Those happiness boys respect busted guts, telepathic mouths, rent, scum, pajamas with elaborate embroidered detail. Hang the necktie on the table lamp, remove the lashes of falsity. Ripe plums fall, detritus is explained with a puff puff of futility.

House painters, rumblers, showmen and shamen, breasted bare ladies, fences. A few days either side matter little. Temperament-free librarians, salt mackerels, sweet-pastry kids, stripes in all the wrong places. I want results. Toss some clarity onto this hoopla. Coffee, honey? I make fresh when I win.

Handlers, bragger breeders, bluegrass mowers, and cropshakers. Bunged it on the nose and he lost by a nose. City dirt is nothing. The workings and how-for's mean nothing—money from the homestead, superior quality water, cigar stores, two houses, four cars, half a dozen servants, two horses for five carts, a basket brimmed with serpents, a glass edge for boasting. He has word, he is broke, he passes through, excuses the brutes. Each time he turns round, it costs money. Nerves can be raised, friends can be lost. Money makes me sweat—it's the way that I am. Knuckles are not stupid. Tall brunettes doing novelty dances are not necessarily stupid. There are manholes on the corner of 42 Merton. Will you be waiting too? There are little feet across her chest, there are casinos across her chest. Business outfoxes the holes in the ground.

What time have you got?
Is that suited for luck?
Time until hurry?

I have an integer mallet. I enter through a hole, then a door, through curtains, creep past cabinets of bland curiosities. The eye is electric. The mallet is suicidal.

Is luck the only hope?
(Seems luck is just a skip, hop, and jack-in-the box from failure.)

On the street there are hats and sirens. A gut that used to be a doctor. System auto-parks. Nothing. Brazen fronts and a referee's whistle.

Why don't you kill me? This stunt of leaving town, peddling with heat variations, collecting a further six kids, trouble dirty, trouble born. Money rolls in mud and meat equals happiness. Groceries do not always grow on nearby trees at convenient heights.

Yes means fine, satisfactory. The little tails vanished. Bodies are pulled from rivers, treatment centers, recovery lists. Have you heard the *no, no* gentlemen? The understanding gentlemen? The gentleman with most of the night? The gentleman with ghost? The gentleman with intention? The gentleman with the gentle ma and the gentle me? The gentle moan and the buzz of our electricity?

Are you left-handed? Have you traveled to Mexico? Visited a really top class club or brothel? Seen beautiful horses and girls on the same day? Up close, I mean. Home means nothing but standing still and keeping an already quiet mouth zippered.

The coast or Florida? What type of question is that? There are two ugly children above the fireplace. There are imbeciles, euphoric confessions, uncles of unworthy heads, a face to unbear, a dirty sprint, double-crossing your heartbeat, hot shops and riots, gas, three more blocks. Booths reserved for parties and ladies. The pleasure of beer upon youth.

Did the sardines invite you to enter? The pistol?
The threat or lure of silence?
The ease of hope?

Enough!
Here is a new image:
The horses devouring you at the moratorium.
(The grass they abandoned.)

Among the Dead

Those costumes   the forest green jaguar
Her internal shipyard
He, just a single-take actor working with a man
with a fondness for ceilings

Listen darkly
Such a nice   nice   such a pleasantly nice
pleasantly cast   of hessian   rye   dare-do-well
Cotton buds light the city
Stairs

Listen darkly
Such a pleasantly nice   sometimes location
for cherries
for murder
Shifting compactness   layering life between style
Stairs

Sometimes
Listen darkly
This   this   this American Paris
Taking six   pleasantly   taking six   pleasantly
almost years to restore
Stai9rs

White shoes   white dress
Spring and time capsule perfection
It'll do the job
Stai8rs

Doohickey   *Listen*
These   these   bell tower moths of construction
Alone at 7:00 a.m.   again at 7:00 p.m.   with her whiskey crimes
and seventeen past seven again
Beech leaf stuck to boot sole
Stai7rs

Listen darkly
Listen darkly
She
Listen
To bladder gall excuses
To pregnancy   to the darkly tuned
Walking with slight crooked steps like the wonder men of yore
Eating cakes with goodbye centers
She will only be this gray drunk for three minutes more
She is younger than she listens
They said she was a crock of slut
Stai6rs
Stai5rs

Listen   listen   sometimes darkly
Listen   Right to left
A double falling through sick space
Her eyes glancing Jamaica

Listen darkly
Chimes of stemware   outstanding fabric snatched away
before turning dirty soursop like the day she was made
A pearl scar of a "don't ask" wound
Wallets to make her dream of thighs
The land in the moon
Expletive nights
Leaving Clementine soon songs
Pin-dot dress   lime-white belt   a brocade whatever
Mrs Gribble   Mrs Shipman   Nelly Rottenberry
And only once did she pose for the first time

Stai4rs   Stai3rs
He never jumped   He didn't jump   He molded   Posted
Toppling inside love   destroying steeples
the disappearing bedspread   disappearing ice cubes
An icebox scene with cold sesame chicken
A bridge between nothing and everything
A typewriter   silk slips of dialogue
At the center of love, he lost traffic
Suits became blue blossom
Christ took leave of his mother

Stai2rs   Stai1rs   Stai0rs
Like bears, they danced those final moments
Little worms   Hangmen   Cornmeal   Candy
Every-which-way mongrel swirls

Leasing a Phantom

Are you shaking?
Are you shaken?
I am psycho...
Fall arriving

Watch paint that dried long ago.

Lantern. Nuts. Lantern. Seeds. Lantern. Lan twin. Turn. Nunally.

Goodbye to living beside open graves.

There is depression founded by the people. Lantern. There are legal categories, impulse sentimentality. Judgment finger-snapped at 6:00 p.m. (or is it 5:00, your blasted cocktail hour?)

Lun lun lun lan barb lun lun barb barb barb lan.

Goodbye to the wife bones.

Goodbye to those retro-pogoing girls who spit like they just lost their pony.

Shapes of sidewalk, bowling bags, a slight jerkle of the chin. Are you sold on solidity? Citizenship? Material and all of the osities?

Lighting attacks. A whole bird slaughtered once a year. Dirt through which most children flee. Find the pudding and you shall find proof.

Run. Welcome to 110-degree heat. Flirt with pouring dream girl gin, panic roses, birds with long legs, one more drink and (uh follows ah).

Watch paint that dried long ago. Lantern.

Clop, bruise. Burst promises of youth. Even failure failing.

Lantern. Lantern. Two lanterns. Three lanterns. Another.

How can you not understand there is no team in death?

I say to death, are you solid, stolid, avoidant of adventure, careless with trifles? Trouble spurts from both from idleness and dancing. Do you disagree most with flesh or spirit? Why does the devil run and why would you run the same manner? Will you extract time or abstract it? Are you better than you sound? Are you shaking as I am shaking? The further is alone.

I am not the painted woman . . . cooped with my noose in a book.

Suggestive flowers, coat removed before arrival. Inch forward. Boil glasses. Wax figments. People flagged and then raised. The woman, always the woman, in the window.

Open the door for the *to be continued.*

Lantern lantern lantern falling.

The door is technically wrong. Lantern. The door should not swing out. Lantern. Lantern. Indemnity doubled.

There is every reason to hide from risk, from balconies, sweat, tissue paper, and junk. A woman who needs renewing, pigeon dusters, keys, *Motor Boat* magazines, a large davenport, neat pile of shavings, kerosene, a bed with four rattlesnakes, sour-tasting iced tea. No dinner, no show rain. Pink wine and bourbon is fine. A cake of soap to carry to the living room.

She wanted a home, a selection of windows, rare roast beef, a carload of moneyed monkeys. Her father called himself a bricklayer and I do too. Community.

And so it goes. Sleep with roulette wheels and electricity. A fountain for lunch.

I am not a fool I am not a fool I am not a fool I am not a fool I am not a fool I am not a fool I am not a fool I am not a fool I am not a fool I am not a fool I am not a fool I am not a fool I am not a fool I am not a fool I am not a fool I am not a fool.

Just wait or grab a hammer and I think of you every minute. You are a blood hound, a blood doctor, a classified, and a blood train. Three honks on the horn. Car nine, section eleven.

Are you trying to kiss me? Can you hear your own footsteps again?

All death is accidental, nothing is meant. Venting, hunches. Toppling onto rail tracks. And goodbye to gentlemen who leap or corrode, who sail by steam.

I'm sorry sorry sorry sorry sorry sorry.

Blunt statements. Neat. Smart like papa in pink ribbon.

And doors go in and doors go out. The fake soap is English and I don't support that music anymore.

Satin flounces. I washed the car, tried on a blurred blue suit, smelt the honeysuckle. I may yet turn.

City, I loved you.

Lantern lantern lantern. Turn and count the river span.

Wait for me at the corner. I'll see myself out for the now.

Initial Notes for a Possibly Punk Poem About—at the Moment—a Girl Called Lucy

Does she smoke while asleep?
Rise in full lipstick and curl?

Lucy is a crime scene. Some kind of waterfall. The bell on a sledgehammer. Lair hips, future palaces. Modern housekeeping cabin, yeah.

Knife to the ear, ear to the water
Knife to the ear and ear to the water

There has been no English lady here. An interest in art is the choice of a flea to an apple, a queenly specter, a dog that shows the way most well. The dog is a pointer and Lucy is a view.

Lucy is a crime scene. The scene becomes her well.

They say priests stalk the land. Troops of matt-mutt foolery. Spittle mules. Shiver timbers. Just give her a gin—she has had nothing to drink all day.

The spiral will arrive. Lucy is a crime scene. The wheels she made up, the rules she made up, the voices once and for all. Crowds of followers and completists. There is square light, wet pegs, a stall, a bangle, armfuls of scenic rock. A postcard of something that already lives and will still be there the next day, the next, and the next and the next. One more acrobat asleep within dirt.

Grass grows. Water falls. The lady, she vanishes. Have you ever seen such snow? Mountains sing of the happy lips of children. Hold the hammer and begin to channel mud.

Lucy is a crime scene. She wears a crown like a plague. She is luggage and baggage, carry-on and hold-all. Knapsack, duffle. She has something to do with porridge. Rational explanations interest others more than her.

There is stationary and stationery.
Action is never in focus.
There is merriment on wing.
May God have mercy. May God keep mercy on tap.

Hostelries remain open. There has been no English lady here. Turn the orange blossom on full blast. You, sir, are witty. You, sir, there are maids for that. Raise one for the missing road, one for the missing streets and loser highways. A state of sin. A cancer of nightclubs and bars.

Lucy is a crime stream. Lucy is a cabin. Lucy is a-coming. Lucy's made to order and priests stalk the land.

Modern
MODERN
HOUSEKEEPING
CABINS

Some face the falls. None have phones. None have reception. Start making plans when you're thirteen.

Have you ever seen such snow? Such water? A boat so small it rests between your teeth?

Downstream floats a pencil. (Have you ever been this low?) Downstream floats a pen. (Have you ever been this low?) God saves kings and queens. Lucy is a crime scene and you know now who to blame.

Knife to the ear and ear to the water
Water to the knife and ear to the drum
Knife to the ear and ear to the water
Water to the knife and ear to the drum

Lucy, Lucy. Lucy, Lucy.
She caught the pox from The Pistols and the clap from The Clash.

Who put the crown on your fucking head?

Lacking Energy for Further Events, Marion Licks Stamps

A window lunch of excess acid, she is
inordinately ordinary

Vacancies in rainstorm. She is
goods declared. Upton's Candy
White bra, black bra
All of twenty years she danced
Slow, haphazard
Karummmmm!
The lid falls off, replaces

Too large for the envelope
The roadside cannot contain her dreams
He knocks. She did not intend to sleep all night
She is steak to his wall, twine to flesh
A kidney for his sandwiched mother
He leans and she feels almost taken

Painting with junket and ceremony
Painting with flute and three weapons
Painting with sloth and a nurse

There is a ladies room for ladies
She is always a smidgeon late on Mondays
Dollars? Just a beaker of milk away
A shake of a peacock's tail
A one-bit felt trick of pony

Painting with marsh mist and cuckold
Painting with firewood and cyclist
Painting with gage and whatever

Marion is a man
She should have a smallish-town hobby
A share in a reasonably prospective racehorse
Nodding at bad business, sharing a periwinkle grave
About an hour?
“Somewhat less”
The lid falls off, replaces

Listen to her dial tone
Please leave a key in her box
No one—yes, no one—will be seated if tardy

Was Bartholomew a Stranger or Strangler?

* these are the horses * meet the horses *
* these are the horses * meet the horses *
* these are the horses * meet the horses *

* a box not necessarily stuffed with tricks * there are light ticks * tricks of delight * would you purchase a town just to abandon it * a blink of light * of iron * of lion roar * which side of your body lies Wall Drug *

* power * bijou * sand * distance * disease * aluminum * whatever left over from that which is left * do you only remark on the remarkable * aluminum * aluminium * illuminosities * illuminmonstrosities *

* these are the horses * meet the horses *
* these are the horses * meet the horses *

* a covenant * of ignorance * my straw * this this slutterhouse * damp undeniable instructions I have zero intention of following *

* these are the horses * slap * meet the horses *
* these are the horses * bruise * meet the horses *

* I give blood *
* I give blood *
* I give blood *

* anything for quiet * slap * light celluloid * slap * who looks after your kidneys * slap * who looks out for your routemaster brother *

* these are the horses * meet the horses *

* stride around the room * unearth the box containing veal * the box containing flood * the voice containing bone meal * there are traps laid for those remaining doctors * donors * the choir spoon eggs onto straw * wrong * gripe * wrong * whatever autonomy *

* it doesn't fit * this this little fever * of little vacuum * of little surges * millpond rancidity * ranting into every type of animal's mouth * oranges good for feet * they claim *

* these are the horses * meet the horses *

* confusion of beet * the men who weep or not * the unconfusion * pump * signs and singers exist to lure * faith permits me to describe in such a little way * a little store without a little care of the little killing a few orange feet away * Kidderminster * Boeing *

* *light light light light light* *

* I had no wish to arrive * like a wrist in danger or a silence that leaps * the end of hillscape * cullion cullion * is a fair picture a fair depiction * is fair weather preferable to decent coffee * I might I might * I maybe * might * indeed I am * is close * closed * meet the horses *

* light lighting half light * quarter horse to time * near near near * iiiiiiiiiiiiiiiiiiiiiiiii *

a small country feels like a dark alley * a large one so close you may touch it while you sleep * is it the same * is it better to dirty your own laundry shears * in the drawer * by the gideon bible * there is money * thank you for explaining you were hauling potatoes * more money * fist * or rock * without burn *

* have you heard too many torch songs * I need information for later purpose * in my right mind sounds good * in my own mind sounds better * I don't believe my mouth is cut inside * my left foot is not always right * ○○○ *

* it's not for me*
* this this mousekeeping face *
* this this situation *
* this this pieta fool*
* this this entertainment blockage *
* where is Joseph P. McGillicuddy *
* in this fine city everyone is marmalade *
* gurrrrrrrrr *
* gurrrrrrrrr *
* gurrrrrrrrr *

* lamb * meet your slaughterer *

* these are the horses * meet the horses *
* these are the horses * meet the horses *
* these are the horses * hook the horses *
* these are the horses * string the horses *
* these are the horses * hail the horses *

* I give blood * I give blood * I give blood * I give blood * I give blood * I give blood * the eye * I give blood * the lake * I give blood * the arm * I give blood * lantern * I give blood * the light * I give blood * I give blood * I give blood * I give blood * the way light * I give blood * I give blood * the way owl rhymes with shovel *

The Killing

This is disclaimer
Cons
This is disclaimer
Temptation
This is disclaimer
Densation

Disgrace   loss   ginger ale
This is anyone's race   you   you rascallions
You rascallions spending your rascalling time vast at stake
Twenty or thirty dollars
A stopwatch moving up on the inside
504 West Olive
Personal business is cramp   fiscal   fifth or sixth race
Spoken trust is satisfactory care
Would you care to shoot some peanuts?

The horses are approaching the gate for the seventh race
The horses are at the gate for the seventh race
Earlier the horses were on the track for the seventh race

I'm not pretty and I'm not very smart   she said
and turned to one side   made flight reservations
plotted the plants
George remained swept   washed up with remaining questions
outside goofing   foolish showdowns
chomping steak and asparagus another twenty miles away
Wife! Wife!

A hot dog stand may move an inch. This is vital
There is breakage
Accumulation of detective
Sing clown sing   sing clown sing
Sing! Sing! Sing!
Are you sliding or walking home?
Place words inside my mouth and then tell me they're untrue
Chess and checkers per hour
I will watch

The horses are approaching the gate for the seventh race
The horses are at the gate for the seventh race
The horses are now on the track for the seventh race
Again and again

Just horse muscle   no profit   just the sweetest horse muscle
Her angle his own business
The guitar case fits nicely inside a chest of drawers or locker
She is woken in a negligee with coffee
Things will become nice with nice things
The guitar case will not fit in the wardrobe

Carry a bucket of hay or money and you will no longer be invisible
Take stock   florist   motel
Talk shop
78 x 29 on the door of no reason
Hide a locket in a locker   then lock the door
More medicine   more appetite
This is the race track special
No admittance
This is disclaimer
This man has no moon
No equipment to buy   pays only for surface

9:00 a.m. to 1:00 p.m.
Chess or checkers 15 cents
Scrabble 10 cents

1:00 p.m. to 11:00 p.m.
Chess or checkers 25 cents
Scrabble 10 cents

11:00 p.m. to 2:00 a.m.
Chess or checkers 50 cents
Scrabble 40 cents

2:00 a.m. to 7:00 a.m. is peak time for nightbirds
Chess or checkers 75 cents
Scrabble 50

Closed from 7:00 a.m. to 9:00 a.m. for cleaning
Maternity
Stripling

*****

Buy the largest suitcase you can find
I hear there is little space between killing and the end

The Young and Innocent Ride Again

Controlled throughout this world, Christine
A liar, there are light and fair houses
Flight beauty of rock, fight hardness of gull
You? Hysterical at this hour
Rain belt coat clue, rain clue belt coat
Boats allowed on grazing land only
Beige viduity already at eighteen
All aboard the Skylark?
(All aboard the Skylark)
All aboard the Skylark?
(All aboard the Skylark)

Gray, bay, shock, bolt
Gray, bay, shock, bolt
Inscription for elders
Name your favorite horse
I may slaughter and place
between your high-count sheets

Guilt equals sales
What is your dream, my demon?
Slapping tricks and ear tricks, a bucket with nerve
Carry her blistering shame over Christmas thresholds
Look for the swelter man stumbling up the road
The ladder loses rungs
Have you ever combed a forest?
Fully-licensed refreshments are like a shy bride at the old mine-working
The belt twisted then choked
The inherited dog barks
The grass is meager
Towlines fail

This is small

Welcome to Bottleneck
Controlled through the world, suggested
Christine's last chance
Fifteen hundred head of cattle, teeth adorned with war-torn diamonds
Let them smile their god-forsaken welcomes
in this ghost-forsaken hole

If she hoots, let them hoot
Christine the postage stamp, one rabbit or twenty-two
The coward, an old friend
Are you gold, a drunk, a listener, still a wanton bitch?
A crowbar, an orphan? Are you the law?
A large bee on the shoulder of your enemy? A prize hog's tail?
Are you over a port barrel
that feels like a keg of dynamite?
Will you ride again?

There's no two ways about, or around it
One sugar enough, or is that pure rumor?
A shape of pie or girl. Torn cheese, a sugar plum misfit
Are your hands law full?

Field mice know pebbles
Bloodhounds appear better off muzzled
Fuddlement belongs with the dolls

Hello Miss Tyndall
Aren't you pretty, Miss Tyndall!
Hello Miss Tyndall
Aren't you pretty, Miss Tyndall!
Hello Miss Tyndall
Aren't you ever so, ever so PRETTY, Miss Tyndall!

All aboard the Skylark
There is blood air
Murmer loss spin top
Bottleneck
BOTTLENECK
Commensals
The imaginary scalp
of the imaginary girl
discarded on imaginary shore

Dead Man's Dog

Dead man's dog
Dead man's hand
Dead man's words
Dead man's land
Here it is
Here's the X
Here's the spot where the dead man's dead

False trees, false foals, false treads
False city, false yellow, false thistle
False shabby end of evening nighttime, hark!

Here
Here
Here
Here

Pig mud
Sorrow crop hills
A crock of thunder, ha!
Ha! Mouths beetling slope
Match! The fertility of travelers. Hee!
Immediate expectancy from sailors? Ha ha ha

Here, here, here. Pardon him then-and-there
KISSES ASH FALL FALSE FALSE FALSE

Amberoid eyes
Blue second-hand drapes
Small *wit-wits* from the branches
A button slips into place
Three geese honk a line through the air
If he reaches the sky, he might taste little chops of almond
A gloop of dissolving garlic

The X in his body
The X in bold
The X in his chorus
His pterodactyl thoughts
PICCADILLY HEATHROW CIRCUS
Regency, regency, park park PARP!!

Here. Here. Here. FALSE

It's 1864, it's 1965, it's 2010-ty-twelve
He's sorry to congeal
He's sorry (ha ha) to apologize. NEED
He's paving the way
He prefers the gate in that position. PARDON HIM
It's not his fault, it is his fault
All ha ha ha ha ha tossing-crumbs-to-sparrows duty

Vomitoria
Silver birch leaves foiling the audience
Reduced to nearness. The middle, ha huh, of the end
He balances on the step ladder like a professional
He, all ha ha harrrs pleases and thank yous and auto manuals
Shaking hands with grease, brickwork, and grass mowing machinery
The bad Jesus sprawls to the ground with a stick

Huh huh huh huh
It's all fake. It's all false. It's all sound
He waits in sound. Huh huh in speech
In sound, in teeth, in heat he waits
He waits, he waits, he waits, he waits, he waits, he waits
He waits and waits, in sound he waits

*

Yearn
Excuse the quietness
2:00 p.m. till 5:00
Torch songs for Cindy
Part Ten

"Put this on and do not be afraid
Are you going to tell me your name?"

An uncertain no from horses
Please forgive me
Forgive me as you forgive the early snowstorm
May I tell you the secret I wish for every night
against this very headboard?
Whisper it like the gloss laminated print
of peeling Tuscan frescoes
with corpulent friars?

Am. Arm. Curvature
Morning. Tree flakes
Nostril. Maybe

A hypnotist is a church filled with willing souls
all dressed in tennis skirts
Replace me with the woman you've become

I refuse, she whispered
I refuse, she mouthed
I refuse to lighten-up, trim, or preen my hair
I want a television fresh and nice
I want to shout *yes* while I refuse in various degrees
of deliberate mistaken identical purpose
I want to shout *yes* to a home
To a double-wing staircase with top-standard carpeting,
hardware, and carpentry
A face friendlier than a coat hanger
I want to comprehend and decompress some funereal foolery
Chalk-cliff worm tails
The way I watch the way that barns in movies burn
Ham, cheese, sausage. The flagmen pause ahead
Relax with a cherry. An olive or two
Warm is fine. Candy acceptable
Three perfectly-wrapped gifts—only one to be opened.
Her flowers opening from his sleeve
Six foot five foot four
The one hundred percent proof of water

TELL HIM HE IS ASLEEP
TELL HIM THE GAS IS OUT
THE OFFICIAL PHOTOGRAPHERS HAVE ARRIVED
JOIN THE COTILLION RIGHT NOW
HE WANTS TO UNDERSTAND LENGTH, GEOMETRY
WOOD WOOD WOOD WOOD YES SIREE THRUSHES
TO BECOME A YONDER
A HO HO HUM HUM DINGER
A NECESSARY ACT TO UNFOLD

Dead man's dog
Dead man's hand
Dead man's words
Dead man's land
Here it is
Here's the X
Here's the spot where the dead man's dead

Dead man's dog
Dead man's hand
Dead man's words
Dead man's land
Here it is
Here's the X
Here's the spot where the dead man's dead

If I'm happy you're happy I'm happy you're happy happy happy I'm happy you're happy happy happy I'm happy you're happy happy happy as rabbits happy little rabbits happy happy rabbits last year happy happy little brown rabbit happy brown happy happy ran away happy from his pen happy from his house happy happy from his food happy happy and his hutch happy happy and bounded happy happy through a hole happy in the fence happy happy and he fled happy happy and he bounced happy happy to the park happy happy dodged the foxes happy happy and now happy happy every month happy when I stroll happy by the flowers happy happy and the trees happy happy there are more happy happy more mushroom brown rabbits happy happy less grey happy happy rabbits happy happy rabbits looking all happy happy in my eyes happy happy in my eyes happy happy happy happy in my eyes happy as we all make happy happy like rabbits happy happy rabbits make like happy little rabbits rabbits rabbits happy little rabbits rabbits rabbits until the dead man's dog is dead.

What Shall We Do About Lunch, You Carnival Wife?

Perspective is not what is needed today
Back and forth direction starts with a trip,
the relevant propriety documentation
And no,
your Book of Perspiration
will never become true, home-bred remedy

Cornflakes float on soup, the death threats work a little
A message received says take a stroll, take a Renoir pretty stroll
Stockrooms are the place to pray, table twelve tips well
Prettiness—a forever-thinning, off-and-often joke
Medicine the cure for laughter

Pray. Mouth "ha and ah" to the hurdlers
Is it not good here?
Can you feel your troubles slip?
Pray again
Silence nestles on the coattails of November

Be a go. Be ahead. Be intentional with gentlemen
Become a refresher, a pie of fruition
Explain a tad before you eat
Before the cancellations, before the clearance, the stopping
and stoppering and stooping and engine trouble
Before the speeches start, take funereal cover
Make a girl feel wanted
The day rises as soon as possible and is, I tell you, wet…
So why not pray again to the invisible or ghostly?

Fasten yourself. Do you understand?
How would you classify these intentions?
From the earliest age, we recommend joining the dots
on the shower curtain to prevent shape-shifting
Do you still hanker for the chief?
You fucking author

Nothing is—or feels—so good
Where are the softening rugs below the vice?
As always, we pay for all liquid spilt

And ha ha ha again. We wouldn't know, and now you know
And we thought it better if you didn't know
We're sorry. We just refuse to explain the
thousand anecdotes of decency
before descent arrives and settles in for the night

Let us sign delivery of our neighbors' steak knives
and vulture collections
There is burning
A topsying and a turvying
Empty museums appear ruins to our eyes
You, as a child, would point to a tractor and say "mother"
And, despite the silence, do you really know what you're up to?
Attempting to blend the head of a scientist
with a "he had it all the time!" amateur magician

Cripple air
Totem rancidity
International psychosis neutrino
We cannot differentiate one week from week two
one month from two mouths
Familiar yet?
We are not through with the yets yet

Assemble everything faulty. Sneeze contempt throughout flood plains
Misunderstand mutterings from the moon
From the seashore, the concrete, generational boomerang,
the toast and the rack
The corkscrews, crockery, crab apples, and glue of our sheets

Good bus, bad bus
speed one behind the other
Step off the good bus
Walk briskly ahead
No echo from this carcass
One bone single pressed down

Harness

And he's gone
Everybody leave the room
And he's gone
Everybody leave the room

Beauty is a place where you are born and never see again
Beauty is poor weather, a broken man, a mangled tennis lesson
An out-of-sorts poacher
A drive before cold cream

All these few last days audible, rotteny
Hey, good luck catching this…this other
The shift unhappy
My feet ex-chorus
Midday? *Strike!*
Midnoon? *Strike!*
Let the ghost of me split-beaver cross your thighs

The place that knits and curves
Abandoned mine shafts
And I think of the fuckheads glassing the blind man
Then think of wheat

And she never emptied the house
And she was a plantswoman
And it seemed a lone jewel
Ewes crying
It was like a moat surrounding a lake not a castle
A parcel arriving from Paris
It was like burglary
Almost prevented by immaculate weather

There is horizon
Artillery, green willow, topiary, petal edge
Virtue and virus complexity
The surprise of timber
The surprise of length
The beards of reed birds, worm trails, brown paper mush
Our Lady of the Dunes

Our Lady of the Dunes
Was she in order?
Could she not swim? Not shoot?
Was she already reconciled to the absolute?

Our Lady
Our Lady Our Lady
Our Lady Our Lady Our Lady
Our Lady
Our Lady
See how she unfailingly falls
Our Lady

And he's gone
Dark clouds now, scuddy
No visible moon

*

Walls are oak, paper is oak, ceiling is oak
Cupboards, floor, chairs, table, tissues
Water, taxidermy, pulse

Our Lady, Our Lady, Our Lady
This is the type of room that hums
The very weakest rain inside

Or Indeed Any Alcohol

or or indeed or or indeed or or indeed   or or indeed

or or indeed or or indeed indeed or or indeed or or

indeed

within the dark all books are grey

indeed or or indeed or or

inside the dark all books are grey inside or dark

indeed or or

or or   or or

indeed indeed or or indeed

as search the way to lay the lie the land or out within

the lie the lie the lie the lie the way

to lay the liar down

pulse of paper   pulse of product

shelling walnuts picking dates

it matters? the which within the lie?

or or or

indeed indeed the grey or or the rasp a plume or plum

a lid replaced upon the eye or or inside the doggerel

indeed the split of alcohol

verisimilitude indeed indeed indeed

the splice of lie

the alcohol indeed indeed

the meat of day

lie lie lie lie lie lie lie lie lie lie

strip

that this true story   strip

that this contrarious depth   strip

that this indeed or circulative good or planned or or

there is no sleep without the sleep

there is no sleep within the sleep

indeed the sleep   or fall to grey

butcher pick-up window light frame

life   the reproduction of an actual occurrence

backward statements in alleyways

2341   hanging with curved beauty alibis

have you been where horses stand and witnesses squeal?

hunger these rivers

the way killers always whistle

these happy days hearing then heaving more and more again

trail continuity mismanaged dialog

you're welcome you're welcome to visitors to notice boards to kiss or shake and the boy is fine and the boy is fine and the boy is fine and out of outside is fine and the boy is doing well and think of the boy and live for the boy and the puzzle and smoke of the niceties of the hand and the boy is doing nicely and the girl grips the light and indeed indeed indeed indeed indeed it will raise to dark again it will raise to dark again it will raise to dark again liar liar liar

a linnet sings now

do not acknowledge machines

say when say when when say

lower the rain

place fresh flowers across the whistling water

in the dark all books are grey

release release release release release release release release release release release release release the light

indeed any alcohol

burn

Impact and Scar (To Go)

rain walks writes bakes reads
furs stuffed inside the fist of dictionary
dividends wilt
slingshot memories of longer distance
buy yourself a new yeah, a new lamb, a nervous tic, a softy bye

i'm afraid of copper and sometimes wood

under the weather
wearing the luggage instead of carrying
after a little shuteye, i discovered a couple of letters
that never reached italy

does not answer
forget about a certain problem

this is softy?
nothing would suit me better
i am scared of clouds
scared of large houses with elevators
i'm afraid of my favorite year
afraid of eyeballs
wallpaper linings in drawers
smashtime hullaballoo
antics and finger clicks

there are fools in this room
there are fools in the cupboard
monsters in my teeth since childhood
there has been a bitch staring me in the face
since i was eight
how do you run a mile, amok, a tap?
set a wheel in motion which you then wish to set in cement?

how do you take your courage these days?
is it different in nevada?
how is the blaze of glory, softy sucker?

i am a child thrown backwards
i have a grief net to throw, an unsuitable pan for pancakes
a chocolate cake mix discovered from the fifties
welcome to larkspur, folks
oh, welcome welcome welcome

i am cold
i cannot be killed by kindnesses
i wander more than i walk or write
The "I" that i use is never me
i am relatively distant to my closest relative

this is larkspur
a nation hyphen-wide

there are bastards, heifers, lessons, under-estimators
there are grapes some say are fun
there are bitches suddenly able to swim

as always there is death
translations, rentals, tigers with more shit than sympathy

i cannot stand these lights
understand the nature

these concoctions still stink
ducks still walk
that's the way history works
ducks against a gaudy, palm-silhouetted sky

switching words between garages
that is the way now
the way forward
comically
duck-sure

ever is finished as a concept
astronauts no longer the future
the living continue to frolic
to laugh beyond recognition and disease

are you part of this living?
what part of you even exists?
it's a good world outside, i hear
glorious
Glorious

i'm just little janey
just little janey, janey
a folk craft gallery with parking outside

is there a problem?
(i heard a collision)
is there a collision?
(i heard a problem)

automatic, a particle, a bed that death can find

Analyze This ~~(2008)~~ Redux

~~Four memories~~, ~~four thoughts~~, four murders, four reasons, four pities
~~Thirteen~~ five loves, ~~six poultices~~, eight pains, seven spots, six deaths
Twenty-four bloods, six doctors, five liars, five wives, fifteen alarms
~~Five babies~~, ~~eight~~ ten children, seventeen girls, nine boys, five people
~~Eight brothers~~, ~~eleven~~ seven mothers, ~~four~~ six fathers, ~~nine~~ eight women
~~Four grandmothers~~, ~~four friends~~, ~~four neighbors~~, twenty-two ladies
~~Forty-two~~ thirty-three men, nine gentlemen, twenty-one fools, nineteen lies
~~Four fellows~~, ~~four~~ nine gods, ~~six~~ four bodies, ~~six skins~~, six beauties
~~Five backs~~, ~~five brains~~, ~~six~~ eleven ears, ~~eight necks~~, four shoulders
~~Six~~ ten feet, ~~eight~~ six legs, ~~four~~ five sides, ~~six~~ seven mouths, four thighs
~~Nineteen~~ eighteen eyes, ~~four~~ six teeth, ~~eight~~ six bones, forty-two arms
~~Eleven~~ fifteen hands, ~~four hips~~, ~~six~~ seven faces, ~~seven heels~~, ~~six fingers~~
~~Eleven~~ six heads, ~~four tongues~~, ~~nine lips~~, four sweats, five minds
~~Four moustaches~~, ~~four kisses~~, ~~five smiles~~, ~~six laughters~~, ~~five voices~~
~~Eight~~ five songs, four choruses, four silences, thirteen sounds
~~Four noises~~, ~~six radios~~, seven spaces, six ends, five books, four letters
~~Four rows~~, ~~four wires~~, four bands, five shapes, four things
Eighteen boxes, ~~four suitcases~~, ~~four taxis~~, four boats, four bicycles
~~Four~~ five buses, eight cars, ~~five trains~~, ~~five~~ eight cities, four towns
Nine places, ~~four~~ five streets, ~~six roads~~, ~~four drives~~, four tracks
Six buildings, eight houses, four cabins, four businesses
~~Five~~ seven homes, ~~eight~~ four beds, ~~four~~ thirteen sleeps, ~~four sheets~~
Four tables, ~~eight~~ six windows, ~~eight curtains~~, ~~four~~ eight walls
~~Eight floors~~, ~~four ceilings~~ four interiors, four centers, fourteen rooms
Twelve doors, five gates, ~~four~~ seven steps, ~~eleven~~ six stairs
Four ladders, ~~six~~ five moons, ~~eight~~ six skies, five weathers

~~Five~~ four winds, forty-four airs, tweleve rains, four muds, four clouds
Ten dirts, ~~seven~~ seventeen waters, ~~five~~ seven lakes, eleven rivers
~~Five~~ six parks, ~~six~~ nine flowers, ~~seven~~ twenty-eight trees, five rocks
~~Five~~ six grasses, seven woods, seven scenes, seven lands, six grounds
~~Four animals~~, ~~thirteen~~ ten birds, ~~four bees~~, ~~seven cats~~, four chickens
~~Nine~~ twelve dogs, ~~five~~ four fish, ~~four monkeys~~, nine tigers, four ducks
~~Four feathers~~, ~~five~~ four tails, four cattle, fifty-six horses
~~Twenty-two~~ seventeen rabbits, ~~four picnics~~, four lunches
Six knives, four oranges, four salts, four alcohols, four coffees
~~Five brandies~~, four glasses, ~~four flames~~, ~~four toothpicks~~, five straws
~~Four soup~~, ~~four bread~~, ~~five~~ eleven eggs, ~~four cakes~~, six cheeses
Six hams, six chess, five checkers, five lucks, five tricks
Seven shots, nine moneys, eight races, ~~seven~~ eight hats
~~Six~~ four dresses, ~~six shirts~~, eight coats, ~~four rings~~, four belts
~~Four suits~~, ~~six shoes~~, ~~four leathers~~, ~~four wools~~, ~~five buntings~~
Eighteen paints, nine paintings, ~~seven cut-outs~~, ~~eight cardboards~~
~~Four cards~~, eight papers, nineteen lanterns, ~~fifteen~~ sixty lights
Six directions, six lefts, four rights, seven troubles, six names
~~Five~~ six holes, ~~eleven~~ eight words, ~~ten~~ twenty ways, four distances
~~Seven~~ fifteen days, ~~twelve~~ eight years, ~~nine~~ eight lives, five weeks
Five moments, eight mornings, five hellos, five goodbyes
Six tomorrows, ~~seventeen~~ thirteen nights, fifteen days, seven hours
~~Ten~~ sixteen times, ~~twenty-three~~ eight worlds, and lots of welcomes

~~*Nouns appearing four or more times in poems I have written over the last eighteen months.*~~

Nouns appearing four or more times in poems within this book.

ANALYZE THIS

Within This Progression, Warmth

To all my own   this cattle museum   I am the final sleep
I refuse to translate language into breath
The sorrow of the latest *ZYX* epic fandango   *LMNOP* travesty

This is the few of the something somewhat better
than the something not so much

Chorus
Solo
Yes
Chorus
Ruckus
(While sinners quake)
150 slivers of broken wood

Cue announcement/conversation
Everything I do, he proclaimed, *is important*
The way I eat a sandwich is important

Do you worry about using up all the words that you know?
Have you ever said words *fail me*?

Applause
Decoupage typewriter
A wealth of fiddle
I'm sorry. I thought refusal might still be an option
When did the muse become amusement?

Waves, dots, paisley sneeze...
Are you trying to spell Ethiopian?
Are you styling pigsties?
Can you see yourself out, or are you always in?
Are you in here, or out there?
Are you in as inside?
Can you see yourself in a year's time?

Would you consider buying a carpet at night
Night falls, the day breaks
The day fall, the night breaks
The nightingale has a pleasant beak and appreciates seeds

The rain breaks
The rain falls
The rain drops
like crime

Detour. Fear always. Yes. Failure. Yes.
Dampness, mudlarks, plastic sheeting, memorial plaques,
gap smiles, slack jaws, cherry wood cabinetry, macadamias,
fish excrement, kick-hem skirts pushing back clouds,
the boned horizon, the end of rawness
Hear those heralds apologize
again and again and again and again

The answers are inside the minister
Yes
The answers are inside the minister

Burden
The suggestion if I pulled the cord,
he might unwind in front of me
The way he dazzled
A swab of face
Brass band
Stretch of elastic linking teeth and grasp
Hands to clasp your neck stitches
Beads of glass, beads of sweat
Birds of glass, birds of sweat
Sleech, thunderstorm,
prosopagnosia, shatter-bone

This city feeling like a stranger's hallway—
tall walls, a place to remove your coat
Wait the hand to guide
Rooms leading to others you are not invited to view
In case of emergency, do you know how to turn off the water?

The bastards are on fire. A mother draws up her car window
Lard, cuttlefish, peahen coats, a dead baby wrapped in cellophane
a horseshoe-shaped house with an L-shaped lounge
fancy wine storage, fanglements, chives and continental parsley
the woman in every photograph, the heels of his hands
the crumpled letter on his thigh, samphire, spring beauty
Queen Anne's lace, rock rose, squinancy wort,
the iron age, the other side of wells. Brass coat hooks
shoal lights, airspeed plumes, marbles rolling across concrete
fighting bear pits of stomachs
the warmth of trouble in her throat
trip of fingers against cheekbones
dislocated shoulders, jerkins, jerseys
kilts, mayonnaise, char girls, charming girls
charnel houses, fetch the ball antics,
belching parents, heavily backed favorites
balloons formed to the shape of bulldogs.

I heard my name on the radio, saw his name on a grave
Adulterated space in flames, door handle moving
Sickness vs. plague
Late bridal smiles.

Here, God
Take this space and do what you want, God
God
God

God
Welcome to the Museum of Cattle

PHOTO: JAY FRANCO (WWW.VENTI20VISION.COM)

About Jane Ormerod

Jane Ormerod is the author of the full-length poetry collection, *Recreational Vehicles on Fire* (Three Rooms Press, 2009), the chapbook *11 Films* (Modern Metrics, 2008), and the spoken word CD *Nashville Invades Manhattan*. Born in England, she now lives in New York City and performs extensively across the United States and beyond—San Francisco, Boston, Philadelphia, Salt Lake City, Britain, Canada, Ireland, and The Netherlands to name just a few places. She is a founding editor at great weather for MEDIA.

books on three rooms press

POETRY

by Hala Alyan
Atrium

by Peter Carlaftes
DrunkYard Dog
I Fold with the Hand I Was Dealt

by Joie Cook
When Night Salutes the Dawn

by Thomas Fucaloro
Inheriting Craziness is Like a Soft Halo of Light

Patrizia Gattaceca
Soul Island

by Kat Georges
Our Lady of the Hunger
Punk Rock Journal

by Karen Hildebrand
One Foot Out the Door
Take a Shot at Love

by Matthew Hupert
Ism is a Retrovirus

by Dominique Lowell
Sit Yr Ass Down or You Ain't gettin no Burger King

by Jane Ormerod
Recreational Vehicles on Fire
Welcome to the Museum of Cattle

by Susan Scutti
We Are Related

by Jackie Sheeler
to[o] long

by The Bass Player from Hand Job
Splitting Hairs

by Angelo Verga
Praise for What Remains

by George Wallace
Poppin' Johnny
EOS: Abductor of Men

PHOTOGRAPHY-MEMOIR

by Mike Watt
On & Off Bass

FICTION

by Michael T. Fournier
Hidden Wheel

DADA

Maintenant: Journal of Contemporary Dada Art & Literature
(Annual poetry/art journal, since 2003)

SHORT STORIES

Have a NYC: New York Short Stories
Annual Short Fiction Anthology

HUMOR

by Peter Carlaftes
A Year on Facebook

PLAYS

by Madeline Artenberg & Karen Hildebrand
The Old In-and-Out

by Peter Carlaftes
Triumph For Rent (3 Plays)
Teatrophy (3 More Plays)

by Larry Myers
Mary Anderson's Encore
Twitter Theater

TRANSLATIONS

by Patrizia Gattaceca
Soul Island (poems in Corsican with English translations)

by George Wallace
EOS: Abductor of Men (poems in English with Greek translations)

three rooms press | new york, ny
current catalog: www.threeroomspress.com

CPSIA information can be obtained
at www.ICGtesting.com
Printed in the USA
LVOW12s1250310518
579060LV00001B/36/P